Give Thanks

A JOURNAL FOR A HAPPY HEART

PETER PAUPER PRESS, INC.
WHITE PLAINS, NEW YORK

PETER PAUPER PRESS
Fine Books and Gifts Since 1928

OUR COMPANY

In 1928, at the age of twenty-two, Peter Beilenson began printing books on a small press in the basement of his parents' home in Larchmont, New York. Peter—and later, his wife, Edna—sought to create fine books that sold at "prices even a pauper could afford."

Today, still family owned and operated, Peter Pauper Press continues to honor our founders' legacy—and our customers' expectations—of beauty, quality, and value.

———•———

Cover illustration courtesy of Creative Market
Designed by Heather Zschock

Copyright © 2022
Peter Pauper Press, Inc.
202 Mamaroneck Avenue
White Plains, NY 10601 USA
All rights reserved
ISBN 978-1-4413-3848-8
Printed in China
7 6 5 4 3 2 1

Visit us at www.peterpauper.com

Gratitude is the memory of the heart.

—Jean Massieu

In the daily practice of gratitude, we discover what we value. Noticing—and appreciating—the gifts of each day cultivates a happy heart. In every facet of our lives, gratitude is a path to a richer and more joyful existence.

This journal will help you make gratitude a habit, however it suits your style. Write in it daily, weekly, or whenever you are moved to. Each page inspires thoughtful reflection through prompts and inspirational quotes.

Here are some gratitude hints for the journey:

- Each and every day, ask yourself: *What am I grateful for today?*

- If something makes you happy, savor the moment and appreciate it deeply.

- Notice the little gifts each day brings—the first firefly of the season, an unexpected compliment, the glow of a sunset.

- When something wonderful happens, write about it later in detail, so you can revisit it vividly.

- *Pay it forward.* Look for simple ways to help others. When you can, improve someone's day with a random act of kindness.

- When someone goes out of their way for you, express your appreciation.

Conscious acknowledgment of what is good in our lives renders us, each day, more able to welcome the joys and weather the hardships that come our way. In these pages, take stock of the things that move you to gratitude, and appreciate them more fully.

What am I grateful for? What people and things make my life better, and how can I acknowledge them?

How can I pay it forward? In what ways can I practice kindness and generosity toward others?

- *Tell a friend you appreciate them*

- *Compliment a stranger*

- *Donate to a food bank*

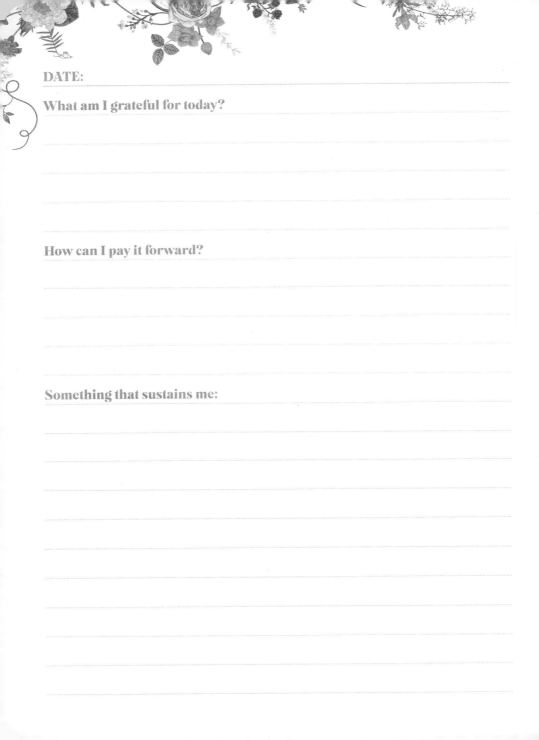

DATE:

What am I grateful for today?

How can I pay it forward?

Something that sustains me:

DATE:

What am I grateful for today?

How can I pay it forward?

Something I always have plenty of:

**If a man had no more to do with God than
to be thankful, that would suffice.**

MEISTER ECKHART

DATE:

What am I grateful for today?

How can I pay it forward?

Something I like about myself:

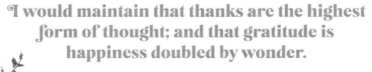

I would maintain that thanks are the highest form of thought; and that gratitude is happiness doubled by wonder.

G. K. CHESTERTON

DATE:

What am I grateful for today?

How can I pay it forward?

Something I'm amazed I get to have:

DATE:

What am I grateful for today?

How can I pay it forward?

Something beautiful I've seen:

DATE:

What am I grateful for today?

How can I pay it forward?

Someone who inspires me:

There are flowers everywhere for those who want to see them.

HENRI MATISSE

DATE:

What am I grateful for today?

How can I pay it forward?

Something I cherish:

The true purpose of a present is to be received.

MARIE KONDO

DATE:

What am I grateful for today?

How can I pay it forward?

Something I'm glad I accomplished:

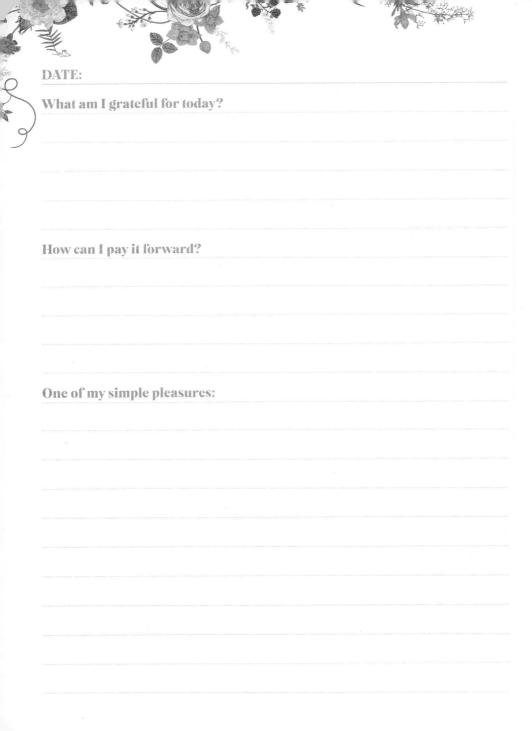

DATE:

What am I grateful for today?

How can I pay it forward?

One of my simple pleasures:

DATE:

What am I grateful for today?

How can I pay it forward?

Someone I share happiness with:

I'm grateful for everything I have.
I'm grateful for it all.

JENNIFER LOPEZ

DATE:

What am I grateful for today?

How can I pay it forward?

One thing I appreciate about someone else:

**The present moment is filled with joy
and happiness. If you are attentive,
you will see it.**

THICH NHAT HANH

DATE:

What am I grateful for today?

How can I pay it forward?

My favorite thing about my home:

DATE:

What am I grateful for today?

How can I pay it forward?

Something I'm lucky to possess:

DATE:

What am I grateful for today?

How can I pay it forward?

Something good about my body:

> *Acknowledging the good that you already have in your life is the foundation for all abundance.*
>
> ECKHART TOLLE

DATE:

What am I grateful for today?

How can I pay it forward?

The last thing someone thanked me for:

*In the end, maybe it's wiser to surrender before
the miraculous scope of human generosity and to just
keep saying thank you, forever and sincerely,
for as long as we have voices.*

ELIZABETH GILBERT

DATE:

What am I grateful for today?

How can I pay it forward?

Kindness someone showed me:

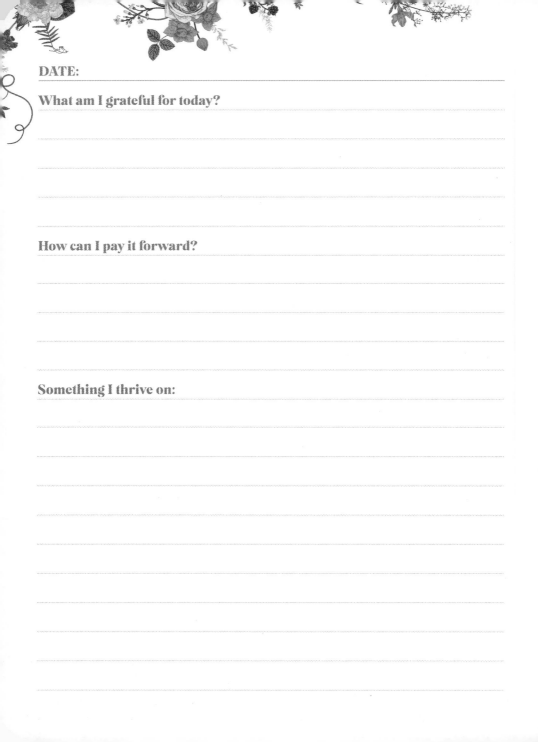

DATE:

What am I grateful for today?

How can I pay it forward?

Something I thrive on:

DATE:

What am I grateful for today?

How can I pay it forward?

Something I don't have to worry about:

For each new morning with its light,
For rest and shelter of the night,
For health and food, for love and friends,
For everything Thy goodness sends.

RALPH WALDO EMERSON

DATE:

What am I grateful for today?

How can I pay it forward?

One place I find peace:

> *For me, every hour is grace. And I feel gratitude in my heart each time I can meet someone and look at his or her smile.*
>
> ELIE WIESEL

DATE:

What am I grateful for today?

How can I pay it forward?

Someone I'm so glad I met:

DATE:

What am I grateful for today?

How can I pay it forward?

A time I've been supported:

DATE:

What am I grateful for today?

How can I pay it forward?

Something that makes me feel good:

**Gratitude is the healthiest of all human emotions.
The more you express gratitude for what you have, the more
likely you will have even more to express gratitude for.**

ZIG ZIGLAR

DATE:

What am I grateful for today?

How can I pay it forward?

Good advice I've been given:

> **When I started counting my blessings,**
> **my whole life turned around.**

WILLIE NELSON

DATE:

What am I grateful for today?

How can I pay it forward?

Something that's gotten better over time:

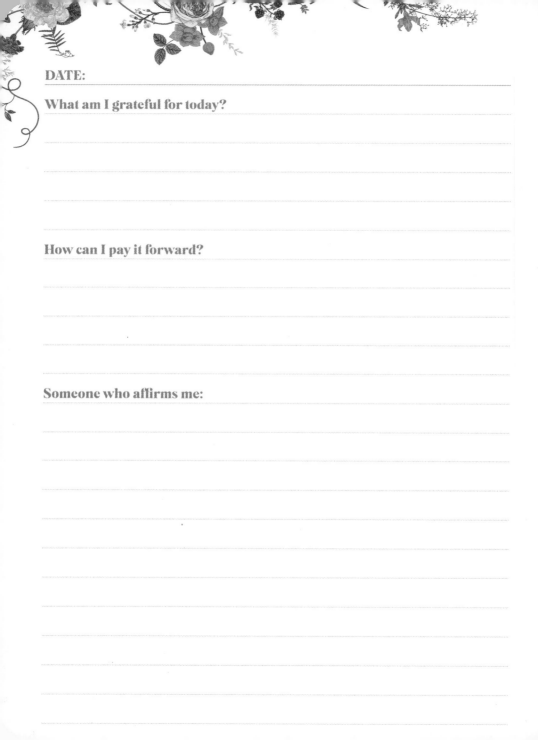

DATE:

What am I grateful for today?

How can I pay it forward?

Someone who affirms me:

DATE:

What am I grateful for today?

How can I pay it forward?

Something basic but important:

Gratitude is a pathway to the peace that we all seek in life, the peace which passes our understanding.

JOHN KRALIK

DATE:

What am I grateful for today?

How can I pay it forward?

Something I've taken care of:

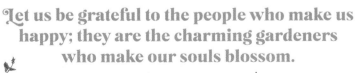

Let us be grateful to the people who make us happy; they are the charming gardeners who make our souls blossom.

MARCEL PROUST

DATE:

What am I grateful for today?

How can I pay it forward?

Someone I love to be around:

DATE:

What am I grateful for today?

How can I pay it forward?

One way I'm thriving:

DATE:

What am I grateful for today?

How can I pay it forward?

Something uniquely special in my life:

> **We can only be said to be alive in those moments when our hearts are conscious of our treasures.**
>
> THORNTON WILDER

DATE:

What am I grateful for today?

How can I pay it forward?

Something that inspires me:

**Wake at dawn with a winged heart and give
thanks for another day of loving.**

KAHLIL GIBRAN

DATE:

What am I grateful for today?

How can I pay it forward?

One nice thing I've done for myself:

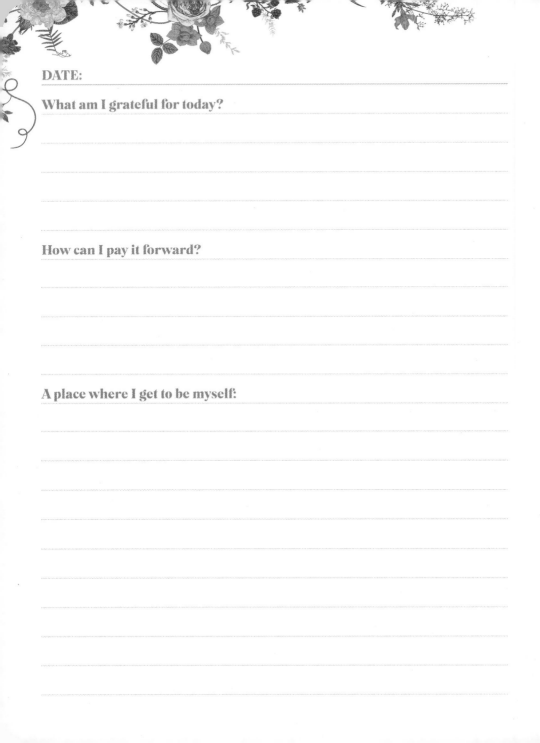

DATE:

What am I grateful for today?

How can I pay it forward?

A place where I get to be myself:

DATE:

What am I grateful for today?

How can I pay it forward?

A kind thing someone said:

> **As we express our gratitude, we must never forget that the highest appreciation is not to utter words, but to live by them.**
>
> JOHN F. KENNEDY

DATE:

What am I grateful for today?

How can I pay it forward?

Someone I feel comfortable with:

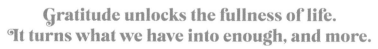

Gratitude unlocks the fullness of life.
It turns what we have into enough, and more.

MELODY BEATTIE

DATE:

What am I grateful for today?

How can I pay it forward?

Something that nourishes me:

DATE:

What am I grateful for today?

How can I pay it forward?

One way I've been lucky:

DATE:

What am I grateful for today?

How can I pay it forward?

An area of life I'm content with:

One can appreciate and celebrate each moment—
there's nothing more sacred. There's nothing more
vast or absolute. In fact, there's nothing more!

PEMA CHÖDRÖN

DATE:

What am I grateful for today?

How can I pay it forward?

Someone I want to be kind to:

Fix your thoughts on what is true, and honorable, and right, and pure, and lovely, and admirable. Think about things that are excellent and worthy of praise.

PHILIPPIANS 4 : 8 (NLT)

DATE:

What am I grateful for today?

How can I pay it forward?

Something that's going well:

DATE:

What am I grateful for today?

How can I pay it forward?

Something beautiful in my surroundings:

DATE:

What am I grateful for today?

How can I pay it forward?

Something that makes me smile:

My work is loving the world.

MARY OLIVER

DATE:

What am I grateful for today?

How can I pay it forward?

Somewhere I like going:

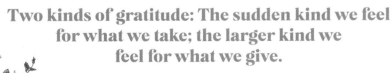

Two kinds of gratitude: The sudden kind we feel
for what we take; the larger kind we
feel for what we give.

EDWIN ARLINGTON ROBINSON

DATE:

What am I grateful for today?

How can I pay it forward?

Something I feel good doing:

DATE:

What am I grateful for today?

How can I pay it forward?

A song I love hearing:

DATE:

What am I grateful for today?

How can I pay it forward?

One way I find peace:

> There is a calmness to a life lived
> in gratitude, a quiet joy.
>
> RALPH H. BLUM

DATE:

What am I grateful for today?

How can I pay it forward?

A little victory:

> **Focusing on one thing that you are grateful for increases the energy of gratitude and rises the joy inside yourself.**

OPRAH WINFREY

DATE:

What am I grateful for today?

How can I pay it forward?

Something I'm proud of:

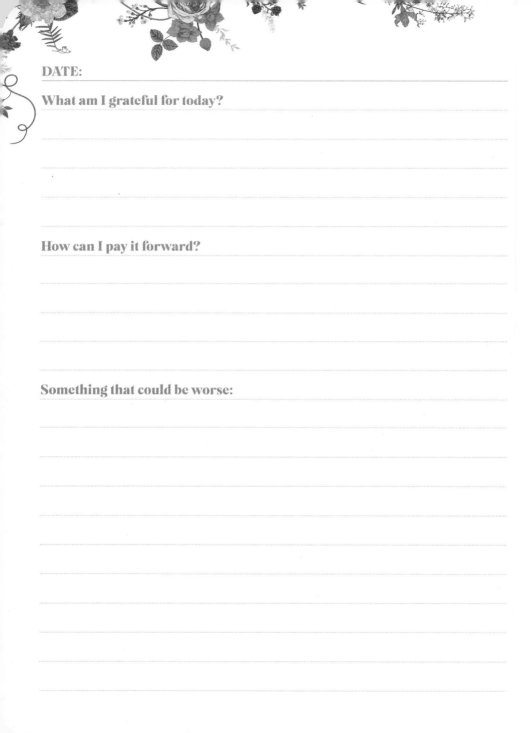

DATE:

What am I grateful for today?

How can I pay it forward?

Something that could be worse:

DATE:

What am I grateful for today?

How can I pay it forward?

Something that makes my life easier:

**When you are grateful for that which you receive
from your life, you put a positive, loving energy out
towards all that is and it will only create more.**

JONI PATRY

DATE:

What am I grateful for today?

How can I pay it forward?

A sight, sound, or smell that feels comforting:

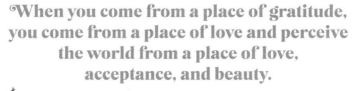

When you come from a place of gratitude,
you come from a place of love and perceive
the world from a place of love,
acceptance, and beauty.

SUZE ORMAN

DATE:

What am I grateful for today?

How can I pay it forward?

A goal that drives me:

DATE:

What am I grateful for today?

How can I pay it forward?

Something that motivates me:

DATE:

What am I grateful for today?

How can I pay it forward?

Someone who's made me better:

Our inner happiness depends not on what
we experience but on the degree of our gratitude.

ALBERT SCHWEITZER

DATE:

What am I grateful for today?

How can I pay it forward?

Someone I love talking to:

Gratitude acknowledges connection. ...
When we contemplate our place in the intricate,
interdependent network of life,
we feel wonder and joy.

ROBERT A. EMMONS

DATE:

What am I grateful for today?

How can I pay it forward?

Something I'm part of that's bigger than me:

DATE: _____

What am I grateful for today?

How can I pay it forward?

Someone who's encouraged me:

DATE:

What am I grateful for today?

How can I pay it forward?

One way I think I've improved:

Watch over all these things: the honey and the bee sting, the bitter and the sweet.

NAOMI SHEMER

DATE: _____

What am I grateful for today?

_____

_____

_____

_____

How can I pay it forward?

_____

_____

_____

_____

Something I have now that I used to want:

_____

_____

_____

_____

_____

_____

Enjoy the little things, for one day you may look back and realize they were the big things.

ROBERT BRAULT

DATE:

What am I grateful for today?

How can I pay it forward?

Something small I appreciate:

DATE:

What am I grateful for today?

How can I pay it forward?

Something that keeps me going:

DATE:

What am I grateful for today?

How can I pay it forward?

Something new and exciting:

**This is a wonderful day. I've never
seen this one before.**

MAYA ANGELOU

DATE:

What am I grateful for today?

How can I pay it forward?

Something I remember fondly:

Showing gratitude is one of the simplest yet most powerful things humans can do for each other.

RANDY PAUSCH

DATE:

What am I grateful for today?

How can I pay it forward?

Someone who's helped me:

DATE:

What am I grateful for today?

How can I pay it forward?

One way I've lucked out:

DATE:

What am I grateful for today?

How can I pay it forward?

Something I've accomplished:

Let the thankful heart sweep through the day and,
as the magnet finds the iron, so it will find,
in every hour, some heavenly blessings!

HENRY WARD BEECHER

DATE:

What am I grateful for today?

How can I pay it forward?

Something wonderful I've been given:

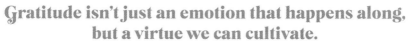

Gratitude isn't just an emotion that happens along, but a virtue we can cultivate.

ROBERT A. EMMONS

DATE:

What am I grateful for today?

How can I pay it forward?

Something hard I've overcome:

DATE:

What am I grateful for today?

How can I pay it forward?

Something I feel prepared for:

DATE:

What am I grateful for today?

How can I pay it forward?

Something I'm great at:

Celebration is my attitude, unconditional to what life brings.

OSHO

DATE:

What am I grateful for today?

How can I pay it forward?

Something I like about my face:

**"Yes, you and I should count our blessings,
but we should also make them count!"**

NEAL A. MAXWELL

DATE:

What am I grateful for today?

How can I pay it forward?

Something I've done that mattered:

DATE:

What am I grateful for today?

How can I pay it forward?

Something I handled well:

DATE:

What am I grateful for today?

How can I pay it forward?

Something that made me laugh:

Think lightly of yourself and deeply
of the world.

MIYAMOTO MUSASHI

DATE:

What am I grateful for today?

How can I pay it forward?

Something that soothes me:

*Happiness cannot be traveled to, owned,
worn, or consumed. Happiness is the spiritual
experience of living every minute
with love, grace, and gratitude.*

DENIS WAITLEY

DATE:

What am I grateful for today?

How can I pay it forward?

A memory I treasure:

DATE:

What am I grateful for today?

How can I pay it forward?

Something that protects me:

DATE: _____

What am I grateful for today?

_____

_____

_____

How can I pay it forward?

_____

_____

_____

Something I can protect:

_____

_____

_____

_____

_____

**Thanks for this day, for all birds safe in their nests,
for whatever this is, for life.**

BARBARA KINGSOLVER

DATE:

What am I grateful for today?

How can I pay it forward?

Something simple yet satisfying:

There are lots of things to see, unwrapped
gifts and free surprises.

ANNIE DILLARD

DATE:

What am I grateful for today?

How can I pay it forward?

An opportunity I didn't expect:

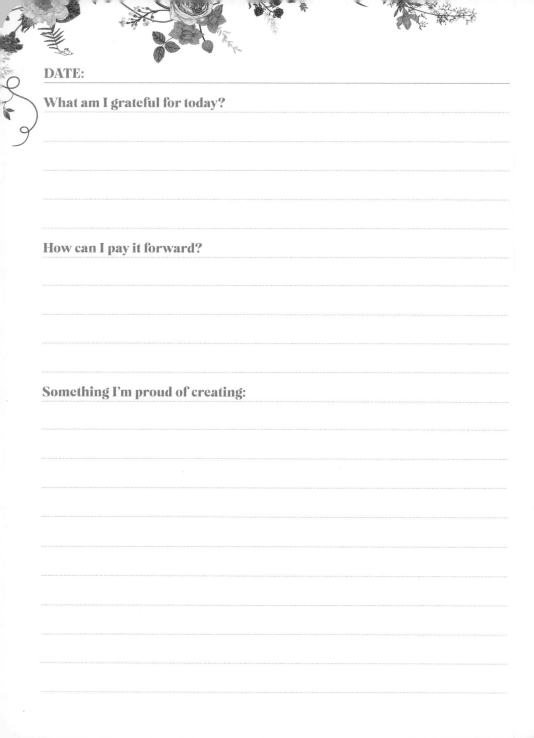

DATE: _____

What am I grateful for today?

_____

_____

_____

_____

How can I pay it forward?

_____

_____

_____

Something I'm proud of creating:

_____

_____

_____

_____

_____

_____

_____

DATE:

What am I grateful for today?

How can I pay it forward?

A dream I'm closer to:

O to have my life henceforth a
poem of new joys!

WALT WHITMAN

DATE:

What am I grateful for today?

How can I pay it forward?

Something delicious I ate:

> **Reflect upon your present blessings, of which every man has plenty; not on your past misfortunes, of which all men have some.**
>
> CHARLES DICKENS

DATE:

What am I grateful for today?

How can I pay it forward?

Something that worked out for the best:

DATE:

What am I grateful for today?

How can I pay it forward?

Something I consistently enjoy:

DATE:

What am I grateful for today?

How can I pay it forward?

Someone who's come through for me:

**Because we are all a great deal luckier than
we realize, we usually get what we want—
or near enough.**

ROALD DAHL

DATE:

What am I grateful for today?

How can I pay it forward?

Kind words I heard:

*Those who bring sunshine into the lives of
others cannot keep it from themselves.*

J. M. BARRIE

DATE:

What am I grateful for today?

How can I pay it forward?

Something I'm glad exists:

DATE:

What am I grateful for today?

How can I pay it forward?

Something that brings me peace:

DATE: _____

What am I grateful for today?

_____
_____
_____
_____

How can I pay it forward?

_____
_____
_____
_____

A lesson I'm glad I learned:

_____
_____
_____
_____
_____
_____

Gratitude is a divine emotion: it fills the heart, but not to bursting; it warms it, but not to fever.

CHARLOTTE BRONTË

DATE:

What am I grateful for today?

How can I pay it forward?

Something in nature I value:

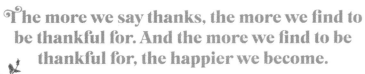

The more we say thanks, the more we find to
be thankful for. And the more we find to be
thankful for, the happier we become.

DOUGLAS WOOD

DATE:

What am I grateful for today?

How can I pay it forward?

One way I'm happier now than I was:

DATE:

What am I grateful for today?

How can I pay it forward?

One way I feel connected to others:

DATE:

What am I grateful for today?

How can I pay it forward?

A sweet memory:

> In ordinary life, we hardly realize that we
> receive a great deal more than we give, and that
> it is only with gratitude that life becomes rich.

DIETRICH BONHOEFFER

DATE:

What am I grateful for today?

How can I pay it forward?

One way I feel strong:

Gratitude is not only the greatest of virtues, but the parent of all others.

CICERO

DATE:

What am I grateful for today?

How can I pay it forward?

Something I'm glad I can share:

DATE:

What am I grateful for today?

How can I pay it forward?

Something that's changed for the better:

DATE:

What am I grateful for today?

How can I pay it forward?

Somewhere I'm lucky I traveled:

Life is precious ... each day is a gift.
MERYL STREEP

DATE:

What am I grateful for today?

How can I pay it forward?

Something I look forward to:

Gratitude is a powerful catalyst for
happiness. It's the spark that lights
a fire of joy in your soul.

AMY COLLETTE

DATE:

What am I grateful for today?

How can I pay it forward?

One simple comfort:

DATE:

What am I grateful for today?

How can I pay it forward?

Someone I admire:

DATE:

What am I grateful for today?

How can I pay it forward?

A beautiful sight:

Gratitude bestows reverence, allowing us to encounter everyday epiphanies, those transcendent moments of awe that change forever how we experience life and the world.

SARAH BAN BREATHNACH

DATE:

What am I grateful for today?

How can I pay it forward?

A time I feel like I can be myself:

Gratitude is the closest thing to beauty manifested in an emotion.

MINDY KALING

DATE:

What am I grateful for today?

How can I pay it forward?

Someone I'm lucky to know:

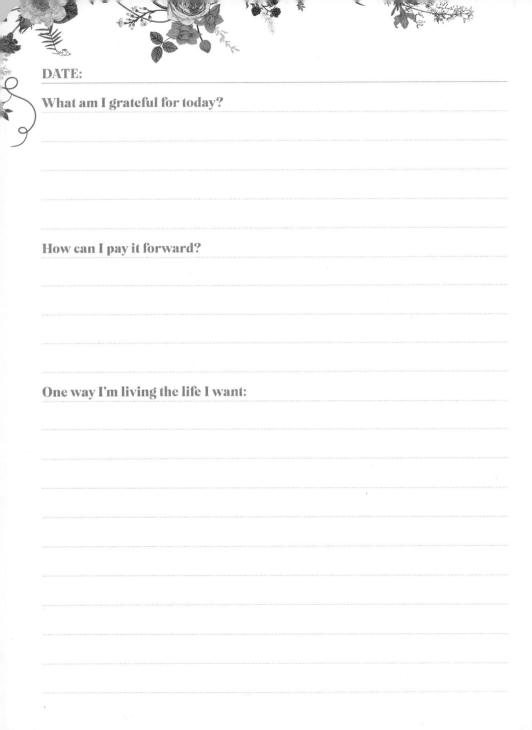

DATE:

What am I grateful for today?

How can I pay it forward?

One way I'm living the life I want:

DATE:

What am I grateful for today?

How can I pay it forward?

A kindness I'll always remember:

Gratitude opens the door, the power,
the wisdom, the creativity of the universe.
You open the door through gratitude.

DEEPAK CHOPRA

DATE:

What am I grateful for today?

How can I pay it forward?

Something I'll never get tired of:

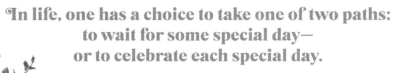

*In life, one has a choice to take one of two paths:
to wait for some special day—
or to celebrate each special day.*

RASHEED OGUNLARU

DATE:

What am I grateful for today?

How can I pay it forward?

Something that calms me:

DATE:

What am I grateful for today?

How can I pay it forward?

Someone who lifts my spirits:

DATE:

What am I grateful for today?

How can I pay it forward?

A community I'm glad I'm part of:

He who receives a benefit with gratitude, repays the first installment of it.

SENECA THE YOUNGER

DATE:

What am I grateful for today?

How can I pay it forward?

An opportunity I made the most of:

Gratitude is riches. Complaint is poverty.

DORIS DAY

DATE:

What am I grateful for today?

How can I pay it forward?

One problem I'm glad I don't have:

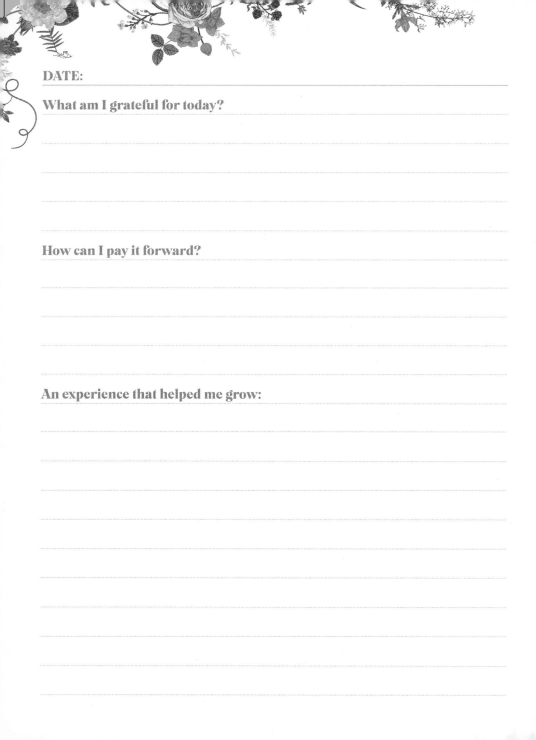

DATE:

What am I grateful for today?

How can I pay it forward?

An experience that helped me grow:

DATE:

What am I grateful for today?

How can I pay it forward?

The best part of my day:

Living in a state of gratitude is the gateway to grace.

ARIANNA HUFFINGTON

DATE:

What am I grateful for today?

How can I pay it forward?

Something that keeps me going:

The heart is like a garden...
what will you plant there?

JACK KORNFIELD

DATE:

What am I grateful for today?

How can I pay it forward?

Something that's gone better than I expected:

DATE:

What am I grateful for today?

How can I pay it forward?

The best teacher I ever had:

DATE:

What am I grateful for today?

How can I pay it forward?

Something I can rely on:

> *I awoke this morning with devout thanksgiving for my friends, the old and the new.*
>
> RALPH WALDO EMERSON

DATE: _____

What am I grateful for today?

_____

_____

_____

_____

How can I pay it forward?

_____

_____

_____

Someone I'm truly close to:

_____

_____

_____

_____

_____

If you stopped yourself every single time you were about to say, "I have to" and changed it to "I get to," it might change your entire experience.

KRISTIN ARMSTRONG

DATE:

What am I grateful for today?

How can I pay it forward?

One thing that keeps me grounded:

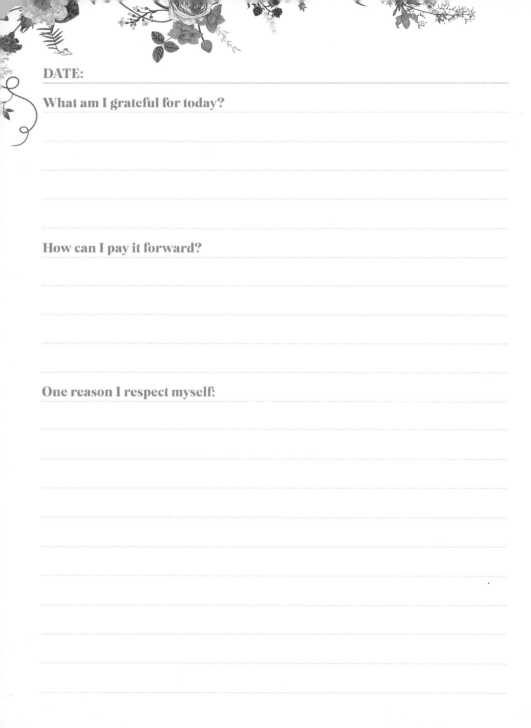

DATE: _____

What am I grateful for today?

_____

_____

_____

_____

How can I pay it forward?

_____

_____

_____

_____

One reason I respect myself:

_____

_____

_____

_____

_____

_____

_____

_____

DATE:

What am I grateful for today?

How can I pay it forward?

Something to celebrate:

❝I am learning every day to allow the space between where I am and where I want to be to inspire me.

TRACEE ELLIS ROSS

DATE:

What am I grateful for today?

How can I pay it forward?

Someone I respect:

**I don't have to chase extraordinary moments
to find happiness—it's right in front of me if I'm
paying attention and practicing gratitude.**

BRENE BROWN

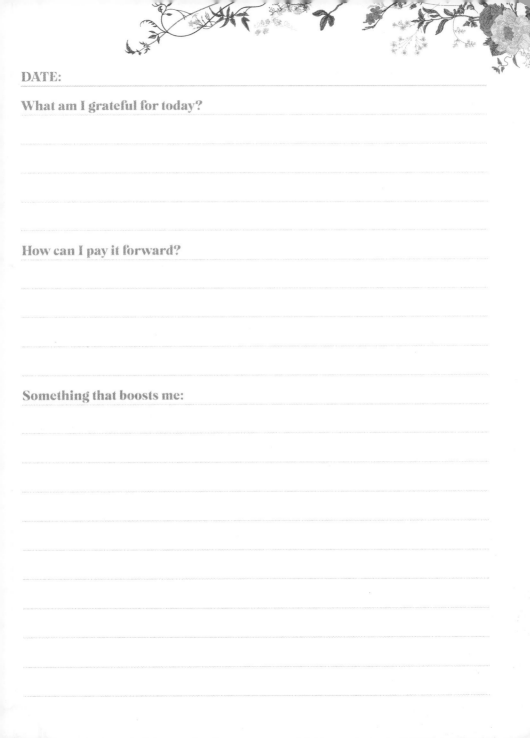

DATE:

What am I grateful for today?

How can I pay it forward?

Something that boosts me:

DATE:

What am I grateful for today?

How can I pay it forward?

A decision I'm glad I made:

DATE:

What am I grateful for today?

How can I pay it forward?

Something I know will get better:

> There is no duty we so much underrate
> as the duty of being happy.
>
> ROBERT LOUIS STEVENSON

DATE:

What am I grateful for today?

How can I pay it forward?

Something I truly believe in:

**When life is sweet, say thank you and celebrate.
And when life is bitter, say thank you and grow.**

SHAUNA NIEQUIST

DATE:

What am I grateful for today?

How can I pay it forward?

A silver lining in a tough time:

DATE:

What am I grateful for today?

How can I pay it forward?

Someone who believes in me:

DATE:

What am I grateful for today?

How can I pay it forward?

Something that gives me hope:

*Make a change. Smile more. Be excited.
Be fierce. Show more gratitude. Do things
that challenge you. Be brave.*

GERMANY KENT

DATE:

What am I grateful for today?

How can I pay it forward?

One way I've found stability:

*The best and most beautiful things in
the world cannot be seen or even touched.
They must be felt with the heart.*

HELEN KELLER

DATE:

What am I grateful for today?

How can I pay it forward?

Something I'm optimistic about:

DATE:

What am I grateful for today?

How can I pay it forward?

A good deed I did that came back to me:

DATE:

What am I grateful for today?

How can I pay it forward?

A goal I'm making progress toward:

**The thankful receiver bears a
plentiful harvest.**

WILLIAM BLAKE

DATE:

What am I grateful for today?

How can I pay it forward?

Something I know I'm strong enough for:

When we give cheerfully and accept gratefully, everyone is blessed.

MAYA ANGELOU

DATE:

What am I grateful for today?

How can I pay it forward?

One way my life has changed for the better:

How has my gratitude grown since I started this journal?

How have I paid it forward?

In what ways have my good deeds come back to me?

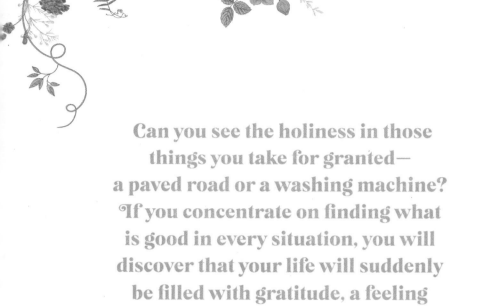

Can you see the holiness in those
things you take for granted—
a paved road or a washing machine?
If you concentrate on finding what
is good in every situation, you will
discover that your life will suddenly
be filled with gratitude, a feeling
that nurtures the soul.

RABBI HAROLD KUSHNER